the pig in the spigot

POEMS BY

RICHARD WILBUR

illustrated by

J. OTTO SEIBOLD

VOYAGER BOOKS • HARCOURT, INC.

Orlando   Austin   New York   San Diego   Toronto   London

First Voyager Books edition 2004
Voyager Books is a trademark of Harcourt, Inc., registered in the
United States of America and/or other jurisdictions.

The Library of Congress has cataloged the hardcover edition as follows:
Wilbur, Richard.
The pig in the spigot/by Richard Wilbur; illustrated by J. Otto Seibold.
p. cm.
Summary: Rhyming text gives many examples of short words found
within longer ones such as "pig" in "spigot" and "ant" in "pantry."
1. Vocabulary—Juvenile literature. [1. Vocabulary.] I. Seibold,
J. Otto, ill. II. Title.
PE1449.W439 2000
428.1—dc21   99-6296
ISBN 0-15-202019-5
ISBN 0-15-205066-3 pb

TWP 10 9 8 7 6 5 4
4500258266

The illustrations in this book were done in Adobe Illustrator.
The text type was set in Utopia.
Printed in Singapore by Tien Wah Press Pte Ltd
Production supervision by Sandra Grebenar and Pascha Gerlinger
Designed by Ivan Holmes

For Mimi and Liam

—R. W.

For Dearest Vivian

—J. O. S.

Because he swings so neatly through the trees,
An *ape* feels natural in the word *trapeze*.

It's seldom that you see a hen or cock
Come strolling down a busy city block.
They much prefer the country, for their part,
Because a *chicken* is a *hick* at heart.

Because some moths can think of nothing better
Than chewing wool, there is an *eat* in *sweater*.

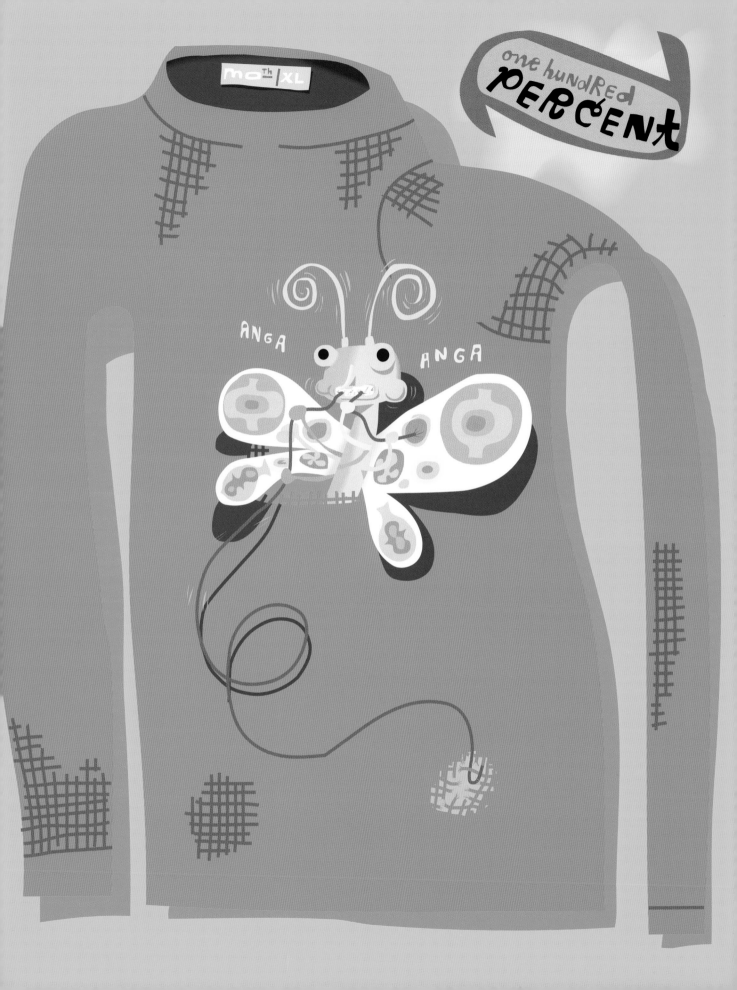

When in your *neighborhood* you hear a *neigh,*

It means that there's a horse not far away.

The *Devil* is at home, as you can see,
In *Mandeville, Louisiana,* but he
Is often on the road, and in the line
Of work he visits both your town and mine.

Some tiny insects make a seething sound,
And swarm and jitter furiously around,
Which seems to me sufficient explanation
Of why there is a *gnat* in *indignation*.

I don't see why a *belfry* should contain

An *elf.* The notion strikes me as insane.

A bell-tower, or a church's lofty steeple,

Is not the place for so-called "little people."

Belfries should be inhabited by bats,

Not small, fictitious men in pointed hats.

There's an *ant*, you say, in *pantry*? I don't doubt it.

There's something quite inevitable about it.

Like you, the ant knows where the sweet things are,

And on what shelf to find the cookie jar.

It's hard to think in crowded places where
Loud music, squeals, and clatter fill the air,
And brainless persons holler "Yo!" and "Hey!"
That's why *idea* is found in *hideaway*.

SPECIAL of SOUP

Emphatic has a *hat* inside it. Why?

Because some people, if you doubt them, cry

"By golly, if I'm wrong I'll eat my hat!"

What could be more emphatic, friends, than that?

An *obol* is an old Greek coin. To think

That one should be inside a *bobolink*!

We know that birds have bills, but it is strange

That one of them should have a taste for change.

MANY OBOLS

ONE OBOL

When battling airplanes chase each other 'round
Till one is hit and crashes to the ground,
It's called a "dog-fight." Is that, do you suppose,
Why there's an *arf* in *warfare*? Heaven knows.

Look! There's a *bug* in *bugle*! We must warn
The bugler not to breathe *in* when his horn
Is playing "taps" or "call to quarters," lest
He find a beetle awkward to digest.

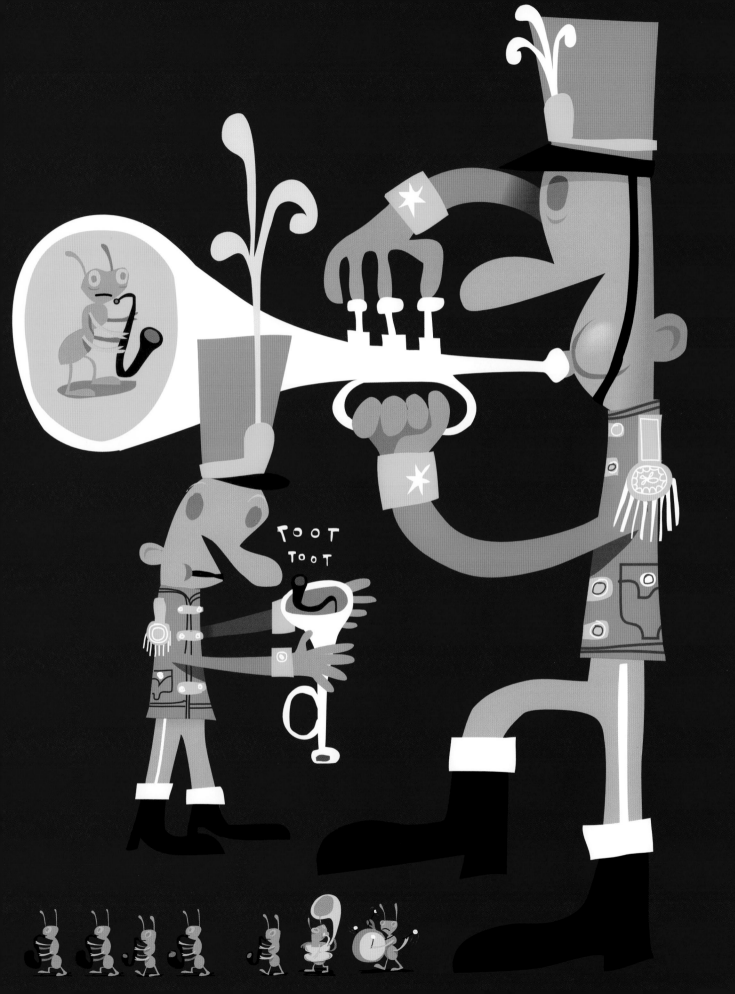

Sea is in *nausea,* which seems strange to me,
Since *nausea* comes of tossing in the *sea.*

The mother kangaroo makes long, long jumps
And comes to earth with very heavy bumps.
That is the reason why, inside her *pouch,*
Her child is constantly exclaiming "*Ouch!*"

When there's a *pig* inside your *spigot*, you
Must not cry out, "There's nothing I can do!"
Be sensible, and take the obvious course,
Which is to turn the spigot on full force.
Sufficient water pressure will, I think,
Oblige the pig to flow into the sink.

If you'd been on *Mount Ararat,* would you
Have smelled *a rat*? Of course. Not one, but two.
For Noah's ark, we're told, contained a pair
Of every creature when it landed there.

If you're fond of road-blocks, this one can't be beat:
A big *tree* in the middle of the *street*.

Moms weep when children don't do as they say.
That's why there is a *sob* in *disobey*.

Look closely, and you'll see that there's a *cat*
In *Pocatello.* Don't be surprised by that.
Cats are all over. Don't tell me that there's not a
Cat in *Decatur, Muscat,* or *Licata,*
Or in a million other places still,
Like *Acatlán, Catania, Catonsville,*
And that enormous country far away
Which old map-makers used to call *Cathay.*
In fact, in all the pages of the atlas,
There's no lo*cat*ion that's completely catless.

Proprietors of china shops are full
Of dread when they're invaded by a bull,
And so are gardeners, when a trampling *ox*
Makes its appearance in a bed of *phlox*.

If you can't find a daisy with which to settle

Your fate by asking, petal after petal,

Whether "she loves you" or "she loves you not,"

Then ask a *clover* to foretell your lot.

Clovers are full of *love,* as you will find.

I'm sure you'll pick the lucky four-leaf kind.

You've heard about that old moon-jumping cow,
But no one, I suspect, has told you how
On her last jump, she leveled off too soon.
That's why we hear a *moo*-sound from the *moon*.

Inside a *taxi,* why do we find an *ax*?

It's because cabs are also known as "hacks,"

And "hacking" is the taxi-driver's trade.

(No doubt the explanation I have made

Strikes you as forced, and of no use whatever.

Make up your own, then, if you're so darn clever.)

Mustn't includes the letters *TNT*.

Does that mean something? What can the message be?

Children, you know exactly what it means:

You're *not* to blow things into smithereens.

The *emu* is a bird of noble size,

But out of modesty she never flies.

Her nature's gentle, and that is why, I'm sure,

She fits so well inside the word *demure*.

The reason why there is a *one* in *throne*

Is that a monarch has to reign alone.

There isn't room upon a throne for two,

And three or four would clearly never do.

If five kings tried to fit in one gold chair,

Think how they'd fight, and pull each other's hair,

And do the sort of thing that isn't done!

A *throne*, friends, is a seat reserved for *one.*

Now that you've read this *book,* I hope you'll say
That what you found inside it was *OK.*
(The other word inside of *book* is *boo,*
But don't say that! I'll hate it if you do.)

Richard Wilbur has been finding the hidden meanings in words for many years in his career as a poet and writer. A two-time winner of the Pulitzer Prize for poetry and a former Poet Laureate of the United States, he is also the author of *The Disappearing Alphabet* (1998), illustrated by David Diaz, and *Opposites, More Opposites, and a Few Differences* (2000), an omnibus of witty verse for readers of all ages that he illustrated himself. Mr. Wilbur lives in Massachusetts and Key West, Florida.

J.otto Seibold has, with Vivian Walsh, created eight extraordinarily popular books, including *Gluey: A Snail Tale* (2002), *Penguin Dreams* (1999), *Olive, the Other Reindeer* (1997), and three adventures featuring the plucky pup Mr. Lunch. Mr. Seibold lives in San Francisco with his family and can be visited at www.jotto.com.